SCARBERF

JOSEPHINE DICKINSON

SCARBERRY HILL

A *The Rialto*
First Edition

ACKNOWLEDGEMENTS

Acknowledgements are due to the editors of the following magazines, who first published some of these poems: Ambit, Smiths Knoll, The Rialto.

First published in 2001 by
The Rialto
PO Box 309 Aylsham Norwich
England NR1 6LN

ISBN 09527444-3-0
The publisher acknowledges financial assistance from east england arts and Arts Council of England

eastengland|arts

THE
ARTS
COUNCIL
OF ENGLAND

The Rialto is a Registered Charity No. 297553
Typeset in Perpetua 10 on 12.5pt
Design by Starfish, Norwich
Printed by Printing Services (Norwich) Limited

*For my Mother and Father, for all my teachers,
for the people of Alston and especially for Douglas.*

CONTENTS

SCARBERRY HILL

Inside the house is silence. We sit and look
across the room. You shift your elbows, smoke
and tap your pipe by turns. I write my words
in my little book. We look across the room,
or read, or meet to talk from time to time.
On Scarberry Hill the shadow under the white cloud spreads
and rolls our way. It's far away. Perhaps
it won't come down this far before it stops —
above the white washed house, the tumbling river
washing the valley below. Perhaps we have
to wait until it passes over. Just
a bit of rain, that's all. And when it's past,
the sun will shine again. The wind sock pulls
to east. It might yet rain. The moment stays.
As tiny cars are shuttling, changing place
across its darkening pastures, Scarberry Hill
appears to frown. You're shuffling papers round,
I'm writing in my notebook still. It passes.
On Scarberry Hill the blinding streaks of green
flood out, the sky's all sun, we wipe our glasses.

DO I SLEEP WITH YOU

Do I sleep with you or you with me?
It's splitting hairs to say I came to you
and use your brush and comb, and therefore we
don't 'sleep together'. But it may be true.
In any case I say you sleep with me.
The action's mostly yours. You made me stay.
Made staying perfect, future and to be.
Apart from that, it's what most people say.
Tributaries join rivers, but they mix,
go to somewhere, neither cares to where.
Both stand and swell their bank beside a tree.
They're not concerned with any verbal tricks.
So, say I joined your river if you dare.
In any case, I say you sleep with me.

JANUARY

Midnight. A stranger at the door,
clutching a coal and coin.
He knocks a bit before we hear.
What say we let him in?

Yes, he has bitter oranges,
sugar, lemons too.
Yes, he could crib a jackdaw's song,
crack it against a tooth.

Yes, he could snap it in his grip,
yes, he would cuss at first.
Blood be bitten, spat and wiped,
his patient ordered rest.

But there will be no rest today
(midnight has paid its debt).
He shall eat grass and sup the clay
('Tastes good, but's full of grit').

DOWN TWO FIELDS

Down two fields
to where, between
two woods, a little

house stood, smoke
rising silently,
I waded through

the grass and weeds,
vaulted over a swing
gate, there I was.

Through the gate,
down the path,
knock the door,

you open it,
eyes wide,
nod me in.

You perch in your high
throne like a sparrow, talk
in your chirrupy, squeaky voice.

I have no idea why
I find it so moving.
That's just life.

We sit in silence,
legs crossed, one
each side of the fire.

You have your pipe
squeezed into your
mouth, eyes

clouded, far away,
looking down like
the crow for scraps

now and again,
scraps of looks, affection.
You are loving me.

Sometimes you think
about the sheep. Sometimes
just sit and think.

The sharp suck of smoke,
the pursing of lips,
is the only sound.

The sudden outpoured light
on Scarberry Hill
the only drama.

I think of your face, and how
I would draw the eyes.
Like that great

poet of Russia, Akhmatova,
they look down, proud,
vulnerable.

We sit a long time in silence,
my head resting on your shoulder.
Smoke rings drift up from your smouldering
pipe, high into the air over
my head. I look sideways at Scarberry Hill, the dark bands rippling
slowly down its side, at the windsock in the garden rising and
falling in a half hearted sigh.
The door is locked, the fire built and
glowing. No one else near. We sit
and watch the changing sky moving.

CHERRIES

Finishing under the cherry tree
we picked two cherries each and shared
another one. We finished our evening
walk under the cherry tree bobbing
with bright fruit hung like fairy lights, some
of them red. These we reached and tugged from
off their stalks. Each one was bitter, sour,
yet we licked the skin and dragged it off
the flesh, the stone, and chewed the sweetness
there as best we could. We'd gone out
into the cool air, faced the wind
and ended up by the cherry tree.
To our delight we saw that, unlike
anything else in the garden, it was
bearing fruit. They were yellow and shiny,
a few were red, some with brown patches.
We picked them straight off the tree, needing
to tug at the stalks, and then handing
them to each other and rolling our
tongues round the flesh and the slippery
stones within, swallowing it, bitter,
sweet, sour and all. We came back into
the warm house, leaned on the radiator
in the hall and laid our cold cheeks
together, still chewing the bitter
flesh of the cherries, sucking their
shiny skins until there was no more
left in our mouths (we spat the stones out
before chewing) smarting with fresh
saliva, to chew or try to chew,
whichever was possible to do there.

BANKS OF CLOUDS

Banks of clouds hover just above the pale
horizon, under the burning sun.
Everywhere, long shadows. I walk down
to Bleagate. Two Land Rovers. Not a soul.
Then the gate to Varty's Field, with Jack. No
sign of the dreaded cattle. We pass through.
Tractor tracks carve up the field. My feet are lost
in their tread punched deep in the mud and grass.
Curving lines of plastic black shrink wrapped
hay bales, then a thin sheep track and churned
clarts where cattle have recently been kept
fidgeting at the gate. Wood Betony,
Self Heal flower by the Tyne. Which roars. I had
intended a paddle but thought better
when I saw the brown turmoil, the stewed
froth of heather tea coiling its muscular
bulk at the bottom of the valley.
Ominous with their heavy cargo of shadows
the clouds hang over Cross Fell, its hard line inky
black, rolled out like a pair of bony shoulders
carved in stone on a tomb. This coming visit
casts a shadow of the past before it –
events so painful there can be no response
to them, no knowledge where to go thence.

FEBRUARY

Why did you make a heart like me?
Big, red, floppy, ugly,
not even heart shaped particularly.
If you prop me on the picture rail I'll flop.
If I'm pinned above the TV I'll be binned
within a day or two, you'll see.

Tomorrow is St Valentine's Day.
I have made my Valentine –
a huge but imperfect heart
wrapped in string,
labelled 'to' and 'from'.
A big red heart,
in brown paper and red crêpe.

How did you make a heart like me?
Big, red, floppy, ugly,
not even heart shaped particularly.
If you prop me on the picture rail I'll flop.
If I'm pinned above the TV I'll be binned
within a day or two, you'll see.

I smoothed the brown paper
on the kitchen table, folded it in two,
drew a half heart shape,
cut it out, and opened it,
then with another,
slightly bigger, in red crêpe,
hapt the brown heart,
folded down the edges
and stuck it with glue.
Rather messy,
but it does look like a heart.
I wrote a message
in pencil on the back,
then rolled up the lot
and tied it with string.

What will you do with a heart like me?
Big, red, floppy, ugly,
not even heart shaped particularly.
If you prop me on the picture rail I'll flop.
If I'm pinned above the TV I'll be binned
within a day or two, you'll see.

HE WEARS HIS OWL GLASSES

He wears his owl glasses, holds out the paper
spread to the sports or business, frowns
with the effort of concentration against
a tide of feeling. He doesn't know whether

he can resolve this one. All he wants is peace.
The peace of rabbits scrabbling in the wood,
dove pigeons in the morning cool,
the sheep in knee high grass

waiting for the feed to arrive of a morning,
crying if it is cold, with maybe two hens
clacking about, a jackdaw scooting the hen
house, and his true love always smiling.

MARCH

'I heard the owl hoot this morning,
from the haunted farm come down
to the wood.'   D.D.

Wherever you fly, whatever you do,
perched on the sheep pen, hid in the reeds
near the sheep with your mate, or soaring as two,
eyes down for your food,

though he made up his mind to leave that day,
the thirteenth of March – what's more, Friday –
and we kissed goodbye as though for all eternity
(which it came to be),

and I was alone in the haunted house
(and slammed the door as I left to go
down the field through the dark March cold of night),
and you visited – twice,

and the geese led me on a wild goose chase,
for I'd let them out – big mistake –
seen wonderful sight of wings in flight,
mysterious, white,

and you visit me now, swoop over my head,
seven times circling, wings outspread,
and we scrutinize each the other's face
through your ruffled hood,

I'm at the top of the world here, brought by you
with your feathered claws gripped tight at my breast,
your knowing eyes turned round to look
at mine and the rest of the world,

and around us the fells on all four sides –
Cross Fell, Middle Fell, Clarghyll Head, Gilderdale,
and the Horse Pasture at the edge of the world –
all face, never meet.

YOU'VE SEEN MY HANDS

You've seen my hands: what story should you tell
our visitors, who will see them too and ask
about the scratches? Oh yes, I know very well
that you can see them. I do not attempt to mask
them, though I've wiped the blood away. They're new,
there's a fresh crop every day when I return
from the caravan. I would not lie to you,
but hide my face and laugh (no explanation,
though, pressed, I'd tell you all) at your
inevitable enquiries. Then you nod
and smile, and knowledge flickers round your eyes,
I don't know how – it wasn't there before.
You know, and know I know you do. But I've not
broken the spell, either with truth or lies.

WE SHOULDN'T RAISE OUR HOPES

'We shouldn't raise our hopes too high.'
                                    Too late!
We shouldn't think of hoping them at all.
We get cut up about much smaller things.
Hope can cut too short or long, allows
for disappointment. If it happens, well
and good. I won't exclude it, yet would think
our life had entered fresh scenarios
in which fresh hopes and disappointments might
torment us. Let's be happy with the things
we know to be with ease attainable,
and yet (we have enough of them, God knows)
persist in hoping just a little bit.
It's only human, but it's still a shame
to let in thoughts of loss when life's all gain.

HOLY NICK

His bottom is gleaming and new
like a gun in its case. Showing
their bodies to each other cross-
ing the landing at night when they
can't wait any longer before
they make a run for it, he says,
because he's got his hand on the
bathroom knob, 'I was just going
to clean my peggy-weggies' (she
has said she's going for cocoa),
at which point she comes on (period
starts) and Nick (ignorant) says 'Oh!
You've cut yourself! Can I put a
hanky panky on it?' That's when
he realizes that he has got
no clothes on! He goes to his pock-
ets and his hand flies straight through his
ethereal plus-fours and his
neatly clipped finger nails strike him
smartly on the zenith of his
widdle. Does he scream in pain? Oh
no, not Saint Nick. He throttles back
a groan. Meanwhile the gorgeous Fan
reaches out in search for light and
the kitchen door knob (for cocoa),
the latter of which seems to have
taken on a spongey feel which,
when she pulls and turns it, seems still
to be in metamorphosis
and, regaining its familiar
wooden firmness, appears to have
accoutrements and to flap up
and down. Back to the startled Nick,
whose pain is becoming mixed with
a mounting sense of panic as
he realizes the virgin from
the bedroom next door has mis-
taken the kitchen door knob for
the end of his dick (or vice versa).

SLEEPWALKER

Laughing as I sleep I see you come
to wake me in a dream. Your hair's tasselled
up against the white-fanged night in shrubby
handfuls. Underneath, the streams are licking
clean the pebbles where I wade and wade.....

It hovers there, the blue stab of light,
then disappears, its after-image printed
in space, the shark wings haloing
the bark of the body. Cotton squeezed over bones
shakes itself out in the moonlight for quicksteps.

The tides of night inflate, deflate, like slow
syrup poured through a flute. A dance is on,
and I, asleep, hardly know
the footprints sketching through the town,
except as later knowing's déjà vu

the feet that blindly dodge the gaps
and estimate precisely turns
which lead where no one thinks of following,
the yards where stuffed refuse bags, dented
dustbins bed-and-breakfast cat.

Knowing that my dream would fade
I stopped you just before awaking
so that I could quickly study
your face and thoughts: you're puzzled
where my laugh is coming from.

PIERROT'S PERSECUTION MANIA

(after Des Pierrot Verfolgungswahn by Paul Klee)

1

They sneezed on pollen, sniffed the honey stink,
jumped at a dog bark under the moon,
pecked at shells, at a chain of icicles,
of stalactites on a gibbet stuck on a block.
They cut the rope, unwrapped a winding sheet
and slept on the floor, skin and spine against the bench,
under a cream plum fat as butter moonrise,
a bubble, a molehill fold in a valley drowned,
an oakapple or an onion. Then the hopscotch,
the roar. They cut a magic lantern, a cocoon,
gave it a swan-neck, a parrot beak,
a crinkle, a beacon fire, an amber husk,
a sickle crust, a lock. Then, face down flat,
on thistle down, breathed vapour,
chalked the nuts and bolts and scraped the cut.

2

The tent dismantled, earth was a wilderness,
with steeple, hanging gardens, rig,
a feather off a redhead linnet belly,
the strike of a falling prop,
the bits of pottery, the waxy flints,
the rock like a puppet in a suitcase,
memory green to the rim,
the jeans, the general darkening,
the whispering, winking strike
of a face, the privet clipped
as a pillar monk, with ladder rungs
cut in, the sparks, the blink
of a tumble, of an arrow,
a bloodstained gasp. The grapes
that grew on the crag,
galactic bats, and sticks,
and parley bones.

LET HIM KEEP WHO CAN

Mosstroopers' law, freebooters' plan
was laid for me and all the kine
before my life began.

I'd lived for just one winter when
they rustled me, freebooting here,
for he shall take who can.

The thieves and cattle trooped the drear
wastes and narrow dales to fair.
Let him buy who can.

But then thieves stole me back again,
home to where the fields were green,
restored to my first sire.

Mosstroopers' law, freebooters' plan,
nor I nor he did any wrong,
for he shall keep who can.

But then he took me there again,
across the bogs to fields more green,
my former master dear.

We came to love those meadows where,
in valleys deep, our calves were born,
the best part of the year.

They caught him though, for his transgression
took his kine, and I became
the favourite of the king.

I like it here.
But they mosstrooped me south again,
a blood gift for a man.

Mosstroopers' law, freebooters' plan.
Escape. Return through No Man's Land.
Let him keep me who can.

THE LAMBS WERE STILL RUNNING WITH THE EWES

The lambs were still running with the ewes when we killed
the fattest male. Three lambs and one ewe had been penned
in since the day before (you don't pen one alone
or they fret). 'Turn him round!' Then, quickly, as I held
his head and collar, Jackson stuck the butcher's knife
into his neck, whereupon torrents of dark red
fluid gushed bubbling, frothing into a bucket.
It looked not so much like blood as mulberry juice.
(We'd wondered whether to wait for the rain to fine,
then thought, what the hell, and went out straightaway in
the blowing rain – which was making another Grand
Canyon in the pine needles, a new Hokusai
seascape. We had stuffed wool into the eaves of the
loose box to keep out the rain only that morning.
The oils from the wool stuck to our fingers. The dust
I blew off the books was precious. Once upon a
time they would be sheep vellum. Now they had narrow
rims of sheep oil instead at the top of the page.)
Jackson had decided on one of two brothers.
(The third was the lamb of the ewe, less fat). This lamb
did not struggle (couldn't) or utter a sound. He
was the fatter of the two brothers. We released
the ewe and the two lambs, who went straight to the grass.
Jackson got into the race with the chosen lamb,
fastened a collar on his neck, then a rope, and
I opened the gate. Out he came, bucking, pulling.
I got behind and pushed him on his way. (Jackson
went on to the loose box where the bench and the knives
had been made ready). I grabbed him by the back feet.
This was wrong. I was to grab his fleece. Then Jackson
got him on his back and bound his front feet, then one
hind foot to them. As the blood drained out and the eyes
clouded over and closed, the thrashing of his hooves
continued, a reflex action. I held him still.
Then there came the moment when, with many violent
rasps, he breathed his last, as if desperate to breathe.

Then Jackson started to skin him. First one foreleg
he slit and broke off at the joint, then the other,
then slit to the middle, down with a zipping sound,
and the lower legs the same, eased the skin off round
his tummy, then hauled him up (didn't want him on
the floor if possible), with a notched bar and rope,
to a metal beam. We heaved and pulled, for he was
very bulky and heavy, and his head, with its
enormous mulberry hole, still dragged on the ground.
Jackson set to work with his skinning knife, slashing
bit by bit, working the skin off, pulling between
times, exposing the glistening pearly fat and
often the rosy pink flesh too. I tugged the skin
at the neck, then, with a saw and a knife, we cut
the head off. We hauled him onto the bench. Jackson
cut off the balls first, left the liver and lights to
deal with later, rolled the fleece and pushed it into
a feed bag, cut and tied oesophagus and wind
pipe, then slit him right down the middle and let all
the pearly green innards slide out, and stomach bag
burst its green flood on the floor. Clean and separate.
Beads of black shit. White lace caul. I held back the two
thin curtains of his stomach while Jackson foraged
round inside with hand and knife. We dragged him next door,
still very heavy, but now without the bulge of
stomach. Coming back, we were about to go through
the gate when Jackson said 'Spuds!' Went back for a fork,
squelched around in wellies in the spud bed to find
a likely forkful of spuds. I picked them out of
the clarts and put them in a bread bag. On the way
home Jackson emptied them into a torrent of
rain by the roadside and let them tumble clean in
the water, helped on by his boots and my fingers.

MUSHROOMS

Are poisonous. Not many, but they are deadly,
strong and perfect. For once, by such means
around the silver Moon eclipsed
my knees got tired. Stood up trimming and cleaning
imaginary Russulae, slimey grey green Boleti,
faint red obscured by the brightness of the Clouds.
Cup and ring – you can be sure they're poisonous,
terrible as an army with banners.
Grass and twigs snafflackled under foot.
Clouds, for which we may allow three or four minutes more
with cleaning knife to scrape off peat and slice off root.
Rain spits between the trees. The Sun comes on
a Point, for by the Breadth of his Body, the breadth,
hope for light but have none. Clean off bits of grass
before you put them in the basket, to keep
so much obscured by the brightness of the Clouds.
Fifty out of fifty thousand varieties,
not many, but they are deadly. The dangers of mushroom
dawn, fair as the Moon, bright as the Sun,
fainter by every Reflexion. And their Colours.....
Edible but I won't eat it. Throws it back.
It's a bad one. Rain spits between the trees
upon it. Let gloom and darkness claim it,
let it hope for light but have none, nor see.
Bright as the Sun, terrible as an army.
The dangers of mushroom hunting are real,
those of lion hunting largely imaginary.
Slice off purple gills to find the flesh
and the breadth of the red, yellow and green
lamp. Who is this that looks forth like the dawn,
Bows as they would be, were the Sun
but a Point, a Giant Puffball?

WHISKY

"I bought some whisky."
"Oh?"
"Yes. I thought,
to hell with it,
in this weather,
and it was a special offer."
"Nice stuff."
"Yes, but I've hardly had any
you know. I met that old lady
with the red puff cheeks,
and took her bottle
out of her pocket
and filled it up.
I said
'Drink up, now,
right now,'
and she did, and then
I filled it up again.
She said
'That's right,
that's the business.'
Then she said
'How are you getting on
up there, you know,
at the house?'
I said 'Fine.'
And she said
'It's haunted,
isn't it.'
I just said
'Yes. It is.'"

THE BOILING BIT

William here runs joyfully to
the camera, where the tobacco
rests and burns, smoulders and releases
its fragrant smoke. He says he hopes he
has not stepped upon my feet. Any
Tom, Dick or Harry can do it. I've
had a visitor. The man from Wook.
He came and said have you seen my cock.
I could not speak because he scared me.
They tell you at the surgery it's
just a prick, it won't hurt and you look
the other way, and it does. He
was quite the handsomest of men. He
had bought all the wood, but when he got
to that tree, because it was in an
awkward corner, he said I think that
we will just leave the boiling bit. It's
the tough lump off a beast. The butcher
calls them the boiling bits. They only
had axes in those days. I said no,
I have not seen your cock. Describe it.
So he did. I said does he have hens.
He said yes, five, but he fancies yours.
Then I counted ten again. I said
I'd rather you didn't go near ours.
Will's Thing is the electric cable
wound round a metal hand. And as if
it were planned (de-dah, de-dah), the pipe
has a flat hole at one end to go
into the mouth. What a lot of hoo-
hah over a little thing like that.
It's a fallacy cuddling a cat.

THERE'S A STREAM OUTSIDE THE GATE

There's a stream outside the gate.
Here is a bucket. Go and fetch some water.
Too much. Tip half out.
You will now prepare the smut nosed ewe for slaughter.

Then wash this hogg's guts,
and smear them with oil and strap them tight.
I'll leave you to it,
but I'll still cut her throat.

You will bury her yourself.
You're not finished though.
Cut this ash with a jack knife –
it'll make a good stick.

Rip up these nettles
or I'll do something sick.
Take a spade and the lamb,
and bury her – quick.

You will hold a ewe still
without touching her head.
You will keep the fridge full
without leaving our bed.

Goats have no trouble
in wet wind and raw.
We'll feed her on rubble,
she'll bed without straw.

She'll make all our milk
or her throat will be cut.
You'll keep yourself in
and you'll keep your cats out.

And if you do?
I will love you.
If you eat of this food
that I give to you.

APPLE PIE

He wanted her. So did she spend the rest
of her life making apple pie? She had
wandered in the wood under the high hedge,
so high the light was scarcely able to
penetrate. What was it made her draw near?
At what moment did her desire to know
outweigh her fear? The wizard lived behind
the high hedge. He lived alone. He got her.
She was lost in the wood. Why? Because it
was a fine day and the ground underfoot
was dry and satisfying to tread on.
Because one thing after another drew
her on. She knew an old wizard lived there.
Because she was simply lost in the wood,
drawn by the high hedge and its mystery
to see what was in it from a distance
then close up. At what point did his eyes look
out and meet hers looking in? Had he watched
for her or did she stumble on his guard?
How did he get her? Did she want to go?
What happened then? What were her thoughts? Did she
change with the seasons and did she love him?
We know he made her make him apple pie.
How did they live? Did he have an orchard?
Question: was the reality between
the reality outside the hedge and
the imagination world behind a
figment or were the trees outside the high
hedge a dream while against the trees he seemed
very small and inside the world was real?

GINGER ICE (OR WHAT IS NOT THERE)

Flowers and beer,
people's faces, books,
looks
of surprise,
a slap up dinner,
sunrise
or fall,
pubs,
places where silk rubs,
a cat
or a kettle,
a nightingale,
a railway
line,
any idea
where,
how big
or far,
a sailor's jig,
a blackbird's cry,
a neon lamp
to see it by.

IN MEMORIAM M.B.

I used to think he was so good looking
at thirteen when he came for his lesson
dressed up for an evening at the theatre,
thick moon-gold hair bent over the piano,
shirt pressed like a fresh folded envelope
holding its stamp proudly like a jewel.

We were kept busy all that term, working
on a Bach minuet, then, for Grade One,
a piece about a lost lamb by Bartok,
whose angular phrases he seemed to know
how to shape and breathe into, and wake up
the voice which sang them on its one vowel.

We played Christmas carols that December,
and on the last day he gave me chocolate
before popping off home to Newcastle
and parents after a term in the south.
How pleased they must have been: he had grown tall
and confident while he had been away.

That was four years ago. I remember
now especially his eyes, his round head:
I saw them fledged at his memorial
in his parents, the prime he lost in death
ramping through her eyes, his tall, polite smile.
'Today would have been his eighteenth birthday.'

APRIL

It's April. Light showers (old flames), seeded
by footsteps, laughter, light. Three lambs born in the night
(cold and bright). We feed the sheep. Count lambs. Quiet lunch. Go
out to see lambs, feed colostrum. Plant potatoes.
Sow seeds: chamomile, valerian, rosemary,
thyme, sea holly, hyssop. Up early. Douglas goes
to see lambs. Comes back. Two lambs dead. 'Lambs will have died
all over the country.' Surviving lamb not good.
In stable. Is being fed milk. Later we feed
it, but, 'it will be no good.' We pick daffodils,
flowering currant, shift tulips, plant gladioli,
talk about seeds. In the greenhouse I dig, Douglas
rakes. Put cucumber seed in pots, then lettuce, spring
cabbage, beetroot, brussels. Walk round, look for seedlings.
Too bad a day for gardening. Pet lamb arrives.
Douglas holds a hand up to warn me. It's poking
its black nose round the kitchen. Parked on bum in bin
on newspaper for night. Crying. Stops when I run
the tap. Next day take him to ewe. She's wild. But
lamb sucks, seems OK. Next day not sucking plenty.
Next day the ewe breaks out of the lamb adopter.
Next day the lamb is dead. We bury it. 'We are
two children trying to prove there is life after
death.' We feed the lambs in Billy's field. Clip sheep's tails.
Quite a job. Next day we move all the sheep into
Billy's field, mend gate, put flagstones down. Whistle sheep,
run down field, shout 'Hope! Hope! Hope!' Slowly they follow.

'I LOOKED OUT OF THE WINDOW AND SAW TEN VICIOUS ANIMALS LOOKING OVER THE GARDEN WALL. TEN!' D.D.

Ten vicious animals stand outside the window,
ten of them! Big black and white cows rolling their heads
as they graze near yond the field dyke. They'll be here for
the whole of the summer, to chew the cud and get
nice and fat, for the autumn markets. Meanwhile they
examine their new surroundings, casing the joint,
chomping grass eight hours out of every twenty four,
eyes full and mild, thick from hock to poll, bovimorph.
God, just by standing they need fifteen percent more!
Eye to eye, nostril to moist pink nostril, they look
through the bedroom window first thing in the morning.
Imagine climbing out of bed with bleary eyes
to see ten stonking big blocks outside the window!

MAY

'This is as good as it's going to get', (you say). I disagree.
Chance is a leap towards serendipity.
Proud as a peacock, mushrooming with Cage,
once done, forgotten. One thing to do: declaim
Isaac Newton on the train. Take
a box and measure it. The place is a wreck
and when you pick, wild eyed, the pieces up
and shake them and see, you lose some, gain some, tossed
in the air, from the bits that landed here somewhere,
and try to make something good and true and new.
It's May: we sweep stray hay seeds up and pack
in a sack and scatter over peaty gleys
and podzols. Something different: plant twelve willows.
Bleagate bedroom: watch the nesting swallows.
Talk about being right on! You're a right on teddy –
sorry, tiger – you're politically correct. Butter up my nibbles
and I'll give you a Helmut Schmidt (a helpful flit).
She sucks those sweet flowers to make her voice clear. The more
she sings cuckoo the summer draws near (the red and the blue).
Even in a bombed out city there's a chance to build
again. I do not take my medicine.
Have a good cry. The grass looks extra green.
Rains like heaven. Shocked by religion. Ice cream
at seven. Coffee at eight. Then wine. Then bed
(very tired) and sleep all night and finally wake.
Lie a long time, still. 'I slept all through the night',
I say. You say: 'You are better.' Very happy. Why?

TOMMY

'They'll not come here for nine sheep –
it's not worth setting the gear up.'
So we got Tommy, and met
him at the town cross at eight-
thirty in the morning. We had
fetched in the sheep and lambs already
from the wood where they hid
themselves. We'd gone down to Billy's
Field, looking for them. The silly
things would have wandered through the gate
and the wind would have blown it shut
we thought. But no, no sheep or lambs
in Billy's Field. Then we saw them
miles off, down the avenues.
They started running as soon as
they saw us and Fly, who hurtled
her burly body through thistles
and nettles, settling down from time
to time to take orders from
her master following behind.
I walked through the wood to the end
to stop them coming back. They were
scuttling away all together

in a flock towards the gate
opening across to the shed,
where we locked them in and set off,
closing the gate behind us, for
Tommy. Tommy is not dapper
but is a great sheep clipper,
Douglas says. Here he is, his
great hands feeling the fleece
(he has been grinding the oiled shears
in the shed while we lashed two ewes
to the gate), clipping from the neck
round the belly edge, then back
from the tail end, trim the shitty
bits off. Meanwhile, the skitty
black face ewe waits placidly
like a duchess sunk on petti-
coats. Tommy meanwhile clips a bit,
stops a bit, pulls half a cig out
and lets the ewe breathe between
rows of tufts of wool and sodden
bits trodden and peed upon
by the ewe who seems quite happy
to be held and sheared by Tommy.

TO MICHAEL FINNISSY

(after a poem by Anna Akhmatova)

I visited the composer.
The clocks struck three. A Friday.
It was warm in the hush-carpeted room.
The sea danced outside.

But I couldn't see the sun.
It was chopped up in the sea.
My host's eyes were seagulls
poised to spear, wings to shadow.

Best not to swim under their span
in the sun's blue light.
Better to sweep the ocean floor
and not to come near them at all.

But we had our conversation,
mid-afternoon on a Friday.
The sea sparkled outside.
Shoals heaved.

THE WHITE SCRAP

The white scrap fluttered slightly in the breeze.
I bent down. It had words in black ink. A
few days later, half a mile up the road,
my eye was attracted to a white scrap
in the grass beside the road. For some days
I found scraps of paper, first one then a-
nother, fluttering in the weeds beside the
road. Finally I started finding blank
scraps, white in the weeds, turned them over and
saw the print on the other side. For several
days I kept finding them, the scraps of paper, each with two or three or four (sometimes
only one) words. I thought, no, it wouldn't
be. Then, curiosity overcom-
ing me, bent down and picked it up. Yes, the
tell tale green and black and white engraving
on the reverse. I would stop, bend down, dis-
cern black ink, then, fascinated, pick up
the scrap, read the one or two words legi-
ble, turn it over and see the green, black
and white reverse. Weeks later, there appeared
sodden white scraps like glow worms on the verge,
so white were they with the rain's continuous
bleaching, soft and smudgy at the edges.
As time went on they became sodden but
still I kept finding them. They'd blown up the
lane and down the wood, torn to scraps as if
to hide something, and now laid bare. The white
paper was sodden after several weeks
in torrential rain, and bore no words.

THE 'PHONE BURRED. DOUGLAS WENT OUT, RETURNED AND LAUGHED. 'IT'S RICHARD. HE'S TEN MINUTES AWAY.'

He had eyes like blue dinner plates.
I'd seen them in pictures.
But from where I sat
squinting from one to the other,
from Grand Dad's flushed face
to where his eyes' beam
dazzled his grandson, he just was
real, hair dark and curly, skin
like a good onion. He'd bought
a house in Leicester and had a new
bird called Karen, who had yet
to meet his mother, who they knew
would give her the once over.
He went for a walk by the river
and brought back field mushrooms which he
found on the Flat Field by the trees
he said (we ate them next
morning with bacon for breakfast –
though later when we looked for ourselves
in the Flat Field we found none –
they were delicious). The clothes
line he saw when he first came down
('Hallo. I'm Jo. And I'm here.'
I had said when I opened the door)
and what was on it, and he said
'There's something going on here, Grand Dad.'

ROBBIE SAYS

Robbie says it's dulling in,
other times that it fairs.
So there. They know the way it is.
Let's go back fifty years.

The bargain is that you will leave
me alone to have my smoke.
In return you'll get the paper.
Shall I call you Duck?

No? Well it's the system: hens
won't flock; there is no breed
of hen that flocks like ducks one on
another. So that's it.

I'll love you all the day. I'm not
confusing you with words?
Maybe I missed them. Never mind, pet –
in life we're in the midst

of death. You are a funny thing.
It's alright, don't you worry.
Always shake hands on a bargain –
I want to keep you here.

The horse, now, he's the biggest problem –
he will always flee.
I've got you here, and you're a caution.
I've no more to say.

Fifty years ago Alston lost a
colourful character:
Ellis, flower grower, former
roadman, greyhound trainer.

I love you, honey. There you are.
You never know. We shall see.
That's what you think. That's how it is.
It's alright, don't you worry.

JUNE

Evening. A cool June. Hand in hand
we walk round the garden, dodging
loose stones, gaps where the new lawn needs
chocking with ballast, ducking the
windsock wrapping itself round its
pole, checking rows of this and that,
which seeds have failed to show up, which
flowers begin to glow, cold-frame
cucumbers to grow big enough
to finger the panes of glass. But
there is no blossom this year on
the apple tree. It has been too
cold. But when we step round the house
to the front door again and kiss,
we know it is no ordinary
love, this, that we stand in the cold
and the damp of this unusual
cold, wet June (but there are no wars)
and do what we do all the time —
love indoors outdoors just the same.

EIGHT TREASURES

1

Because language is difficult for me
I have holes. Read the meaning in my whole.
Look at me. Look through me. I am split,
light grey, bleaching from the tip.
My fate is to stay too long. I turn and change,
turn many ways. I slowly lay down
on the ground till I was found.
The holes are all that is absent.
I want to enclose again, to wrap around
the living tissue of the thistle stem.
But it is gone. One day I will be gone.
You noticed me, saw my meaning
on a particular day. I had been here
a long time. Look at me. Look through me.
I can show you the world. I am a petrified saint.
I am an insect with many eyes.
My holes are my bereavements.
Each one is a grief that I will not forget.
I am a hand held out. I let rain trickle through
like tears. I am a sieve. I encircle light.
I am the angle at which I lie.
If I were an animal where would be my eye?
If I were the world where would be my whole?
Walk in under my canopy.
See the light through my windows, feel the rain.

2

It must have died in winter
when there were few predators
and the sheep avoided that windy shelf.
It has opened up like a flower
sown in the grass
under the hawthorn tree.

It knocked around for a bit
on the table. The two front teeth
dropped out of their sheath
from time to time.

The deep lacrimal come hither
shadows of the eye sockets
cover a labyrinthine chamber.

3

A bottle bottom. Light becomes
irregular, in its own image, where
the air that shapes everything pushed the gob
into the mould. It holds nothing but air.
The bottom catches the skin,
is tinted turquoise. A circle, not a lens,
is stamped in the base, ribbed concentrically
as a pool of water pierced by a stone,
two concave shores abreast,
two corners intact, two chipped sheer.
It cannot hold anything but the lens
with grain as hard as the prick of air
in a bubble from the lung of the gaffer
and bent as a glacier spreading rings.
These lines were tensed into the glass
by the gaffer's lips, the tiny bubble passing
across the narrow space slow like a star.
It clouds where flakes of glass have fallen.
The breaks catch light. Clonk it down.
There is a foursquare rightness about it then
which it was made for. It is a monument.

4

A wand,
a bit
of tree
gnawed
smooth
by a
wood
creature,
base
cracked
to the
core
of pith
hidden
under
brown
streaked
sheen
of shaft,
leaf scar
and bud,
wide
spaced
spiral,
pointing
pegs.

5

It is a blade of bone set with seven teeth
(a chalky cliff with seven houses
balancing their pointy roofs, uprights
not quite plumb, jostling
each other, snug and settled, rooted
in that curve; a ship with massive prow
tossing up into the salt air from
the sea, with high on its flanks a row
of battlements, and on the flaking
stern a tiny porthole, a lookout
on a shore dissolving in the past).

6

Its body curves,
scales lift,
cracked edges curl,
afloat on air,
a ragged stump
atop it where
it peeled
off a tree,
flung its seeds,
leaving their
shadows to sleep,
deep in green,
is firm yet light
as a bird,
lay by the lambs' pen
on the ground.
Press it.
With a dry rustle
it rebounds.
It is scarred yet whole.
And you ask me
would I collect
a few to put
in a bowl?
No.
This is the only one.

7

It
stuck
in the mud, its pit-
ted surface unsucked. It weighed heavy,
spoke even, then jumped, maybe dangerous,
different from a stone, all rust, flaking away. When
you scraped it with your thumb nail, picked off a tiny bit,
I said: No. Leave its mystery. You were
trying to find out what was in it.
A polished bit is all,
the rest is a ball,
a knobby ball.
Why you got
to get it
spl-
it?

8

One has a hole in its side,
one a crack.
Neither has anything to hide.

What lived inside
the air
and predators have dried.

By now they should be dust.
Something serious
went awry in that nest.

They still exist.
With shadows like the moon's, and blue,
they tremble in a matchbox now,
in the treasure chest.

JULY

'Well, it's certainly raining today.'
Walking to the shed on this July
morning under the dunked rain clouds
pelting, pattering, steaming, glowing
and white, on the hills standing head and shoulders
over us, shoulder to shoulder
in the vast cathedral of which this
wood we huddle through in the drizzle
is a simple side chapel,
or even just a pew, or a hole
in the floorboards, from which vantage point
we can see our little things,
hens sheltered in the straw, one
half-size egg in the tabernacle
awaiting us, sheep, half of them
shorn, potatoes, rhubarb shorn by the lambs
of the gods, of the hills, we prepare
ourselves for a sacrament of strawberries,
not quite ripe, but dunked in red stained sugar
like blood, thicker than
the flood which is St. Swithun's.

INSTEAD OF TIME

Do you not hear the sea?
Snow still falls on your grave
(I threw a red rose).
The wind still blows.

And we just breathe,
look at the Sun, the Moon, the Stars, the Earth.
Are you now? Are you then?
Are you....? Stay still and see.

Snow still falls on your grave
(I threw a red rose).
The wind still blows.

If we had both been born next century
when things will anyhow be different,
if we had been the same (instead of Time)...

Snow still falls on your grave
(I threw a red rose).
The wind still blows.

We are in a calm. I see
your figure vanishing.
Is there another life?
Shall I awake, find this a dream?

Snow still falls on your grave
(I threw a red rose).
The wind still blows.

It is Time. An angel showed me everything.
And said 'You have no further use for these.
A page has only room
for Justice.'

Snow still falls on your grave
(I threw a red rose).
The wind still blows.
Do you not hear the sea?

DINNER FOR ONE

She wandered half across London
for five minutes' conversation,
then brought back dinner for one.

In the cut glass eye of the studio
she matched blue, green and yellow
with careful brush strokes, solo.

Slowly, it emerged,
diagonal lines, colour, edged
with pinches of warmth, fudged

deliberately, to depict
life, or simply to contradict,
to block a new edict.

She was thin, bony, cropped,
moved dryly like a bird,
or could have been a postcard.

She had no profile, or shape that lingers,
but a quiver of long brush-like fingers
which rustled when she peeled oranges.

Her painting she called 'Apocalyptic Restraint'.
It was exhibited at the Tate, and lent
on permanent loan to a friend

whose home was a magnet for international
musicians, artists, writers of a functional
bent rather than confessional.

She still wandered half across London
for five minutes' conversation,
then thought about dinner for one.

BALLOONS

Another glistening mist-magic morning.
The catering staff were blowing up balloons
all day. Walked down to call the lambs, (two hidden
in the trees). They rolled and ambled when
I went to fetch them. Like balloons in fact.
Yes. Balloons. With canisters of helium.
You pop one, then the next one pops as well,
(the idea goes, but somehow never get round
to trying it out). You pop it with a pin.
It makes a lovely little bang, a muffled
gun (I said to him and her together
when we met that evening). They were
everywhere, mirrors one side, marks
the other. (London, he said. How very strange).
We went to count the ewes, see how they were,
fell down and dangled, sitting in a huddle
at a cousin's wedding party with
inflated condoms, bobbled on the end.
(They photographed me floating down the steps,
a girl with five balloons, and popped them all).
In Billy's Field. Looked round as though to say:
It's Ladies' Day. Fuck off! And the balloons?
In hospital I chased a patient with
her five balloons and popped them with my own
deflated one. I stuck them on the stairs.
A shameful episode. (They stayed for weeks).
But true. The firemen tied them to their truck
(and someone whispered: those are blown up condoms
flopping) then careered off waving them.
My first year there the orchestra had thrown
a mighty party. Very young composers
always have balloons pinned in the air.
A birthday party. (Did you ever think?).
A mighty party. Wore my taffeta.
Then hung my flat with green balloons, deflating.

AUGUST

August. The first fine morning of the summer.
The sky is egg shell blue. I throw wide
the kitchen door to let a gasp of blown air in
(we've kept the stove alight – nothing is sure),
and step into the space outside, the quiet, the light,
the blue.....
After breakfast, the shed. Let out the hens.
Collect two eggs. Cover their food against crows.
Then on down the Flat Field seeking mushrooms
on the edge of the wood. Two pigeons there.
One, nearly dead, accepts in peace the offered coup.
The other has gone before. 'The weather.' Douglas says.
A circle of white field mushrooms stands nearby.
We glean the four that glow, grey gilled,
leave black side up in the muck the maggoty one,
cross the narrow track the sheep, stepping from Billy's
Field, have beaten into the edge of the Flat Field,
the bulge of the hanky bundle loosely tied
(later emptied, flak, pine needles and all,
onto the kitchen table). Back to the shed for Jack,
who sits with a totally unreproachful attention
behind the gate, eager to seek a rabbit
carcase under the willow if allowed
to do so despite his owner's frown.

WHAT HAS HAPPENED TO KEGU'S BRIDE?

Fifty bales of straw, a sack of corn. Farya is pounding wheat.
We sit around the fire, our green castle for a while.
The lord protects our land. The trees grow round his house.
We give him half our corn and twenty sheep a year.
The sun stands on the hill ripe to break.
The hills are changing. Changing makes them fruit.
Days are honey warm. Mother drapes the door
to keep us warm. Fire inside a cage.
Black stone or wood. Imagine, I can draw.
And Farya says that all things change.
Seshon says they all came from the hill.
Twenty sacks of corn. Farya doesn't like
this weaving song with book, the business of the land
with love. Yes, this is love. Why draw what's spoken,
drawn in air before it falls, like rainbow
showers? Weaving needs a warp and weft.
And so I draw my song as well as books. When Kegu
was to marry, children took the small stones,
we the big, to build his house. They say it's warm.
Now is the time when smells begin to rise again.
Snow gets thin. Kegu's bride lives over the fell.
We went for the binding of cloth. She showed me a hidden
thing. She said I have something hidden
where I sleep. I dare not show my father, but Kegu
will like it as much as I. She lifted the woollen robe.
She found it in the hollow of an oak, alone.
What can I say? I would like to say
think of your father, but I cannot speak.
He will take up his bow. She will cry, her tears
will fall like sacks of wheat. I have not seen her now
winter and spring. The time of the marriage is close.
What has happened to Kegu's bride?
This is my secret place. Father, if you find me here,
if you find my drawings spare me, for I weave by day
as well as draw by night. I do all that a father could hope
of his daughter and I carry the pans of food
to the fire and back. In time I will marry.
Can you ask more?

HENRY MILLER IN CONSTABLE COUNTRY

Hell. A sulphur yellow square.
The fat secure bastards curse
indoors. No-one's passed this snap-shaped
window in two thousand years.

Blocks and blocks of cosy semis,
miles and miles of cats and dogs,
canaries, budgies, hamsters, gerbils rot inside
this animal heat-belt, city suspender-belt.

Fullmore's full of ideas about the cunts.
'Mythos' he calls it. I like it. The railway
underground, steaming and more and more invisible,
miles and miles of stacks of reserve false teeth...

In short, we're going back to alchemy,
to symbols, entrails, metal poking rods.
We'll get this gold without base piety.
No regrets. No bulls. No bears. And no brutality.

WILL I BE TESTED

Will I be tested, fail, be punished, spend
seven years as a stone in payment? What would it take
to pass this test, how much success? I'm in
a pattern, I know, and have no power to break
it. Can I be builder of roads and traveller
in one, when building the road is all I do?
or storyteller, or philosopher
(we never travel, only make the road).
How can I query your requiring me
to never fail again, when I have failed
by making a pattern fruitfully repeat?
when I might change it easily enough
by changing the route. How can I ever fail
if I obey the golden rule of love?

MAYBE THIS KIND OF LOVE

Maybe this kind of love is over subtle.
It hangs on times of day and frames of mind.
If things are right the heart is in fine fettle,
if not, we hold it dear. We're not designed,
at twice and half each other's age, to find
the details sorted on the surface level.
Nor can we easily solve the deeper kind
but hand in hand with a love as physical
as this, which goes in hand, in spite of all
disparities, with love that stays the same
in passion, anger, pain. We can't control
when we were born or how our meeting came.
We may yet find that there's a name to this,
a story we can tell, a way to kiss.

AS ANY LOVER WOULD

As any lover would, I wish you well,
prosperous, happy, florens. As you do me.
I want to be (how selfish can one be?)
the one to make you flourish, that's the trouble.
I'd rather you were poor and destitute,
I do confess, if that were possible
without a loss of happiness. As well,
I'd rather be the one to buy the food.
Would cheese taste any different bought by you?
Does bread go bad if you provide the dough?
I think not, and I know you'd rather do
the paying for them, but I also know
I'd be too sensible at this banal
pursuit. So, tough. You cannot have it all.

DON'T GIVE ME RECOMPENSE

Don't give me recompense for given love.
Giving myself I've paid my own expense.
Don't set a price on kisses I may give –
tender kisses tender their own pence.
Don't think of love for you as 'services',
for which transactions are reckoned to satisfy
accounts, but leave this love to its own devices,
like for a like reward. Love will defy
attempts to open its purse, wants not to know
the contents, trusts there will always be enough,
careful to put its takings in escrow,
with no third party needed, only the self.
Reward me as no one else on earth can do,
in heaven, indeed in the whole of time: with you.

IF YOU WERE GOD

If you were God, wouldn't you grow things from seed?
You'd have the confidence in what you'd made
To watch it grow, for which you'd made it time,
Or else you'd not have started it at all.

If you were God, you'd be quite capable,
by definition, of making DNA,
the quantum particles and energy fields,
and goodness knows what else to get things going.

If you were God, you'd want a fair good run
for your money, not a flower starting part
way up the stem. You wouldn't want to cheat
by doing something so devoid of fun.

You wouldn't need to pull rabbits out of a hat.
If you were God, you'd be cleverer than that.

WOULD YOU GET RID OF CRIME

If you were God, would you get rid of crime,
of war, of famine, pain, distress, the lot?
Would you wipe out shady dealings, underhand
practices and smashings of the skull?

If you were God, you'd not want people in Hell
no matter what they'd done. You'd maybe defend
them if you loved them, rather than alot
a punishment that matched their crime each time.

If you were God, would you give them the choice
to be bad or not, or would you chicken out
altogether from making people free?
It's a gamble, knowing what the buggers are like.

As God, if you gave them voice, you'd know the craic.
You'd have had your reasons, known what it was about.

SINCE YOU'RE ONLY HUMAN

Since you're only human, you'd better know what
defines your state. You have some power, it's true,
not infinite: you were not there at the start –
you can imagine being there, but it wasn't you.

Just as you can imagine living for ever,
but it won't be you who's there at the end of time.
But then, you're good at 'imagine', you can measure
everything that's happened during time

but nothing out: that's where your limit lies.
Hang on, we're not just talking limits, are we,
but what you are: 'imagine' is more than lies
and make believe. Isn't it as though you see?

(with what? you could ask: with what do you see? and how,
in any situation, or ever, know?)

PENELOPE

The boxes came packed flat:
we knocked them out, slotted flaps
inside each other, smeared a plastic bag
and shook to catch some air inside,
patted it round inside the box
and folded edges neatly round the top.

>Wait for the bubble to snap,
>listen for the spit of it
>when you unwrap,
>waiting for the bubble to snap,
>the string and paper in hope
>the double and shadow will fit.
>Wait for the bubble to snap,
>listen for the spit of it.

A digger knuckled the chocolate
rubble outside the window, testing
silence; people stopped to watch. The earth
bristled with gravestones. On the sill
someone had put a jar
crammed with blood carnations.

>A horse, a tree, a shadow,
>a house and a block of flats.
>A cow, a stream, a meadow,
>a horse, a tree, a shadow.
>A train, a moving window,
>moving eyes and moving hats.
>A horse, a tree, a shadow,
>a house and a block of flats.

'Dear Mr. U. I'm holding
a small brown box containing
approx thirty books,
many of them inscribed
"to or from U." around ten years ago.
Could you please inform me whether you...'

        Wait for the bubble to snap,
        listen for the spit of it
        when you unwrap,
        waiting for the bubble to snap,
        the string and paper in hope
        the double and shadow will fit.
        Wait for the bubble to snap,
        listen for the spit of it.

As Penelope poured wine
from a pelyx it splashed the edge
of her hem. She bent and pressed the cloth
between her thumb and finger,
sucking as she thought of greaseproof
paper, cream, Kirsch and cash.

        I'm getting good at this:
        I can sew a pocket a minute
        almost asleep. The hiss –
        I'm getting good at this –
        the thump of the steam press
        wake me day and night.
        I'm getting good at this:
        I can sew a pocket a minute.

Outside the factory, along
the luminous track, a train
gathered up enough speed
and slid into the earth.
Next day Penelope kept mopping up
between her legs the smell of fish.

        I should point out
        that this is a tape.
        If you want to speak out
        I should point out
        there's no need to shout,
        no chance of escape.
        I should point out
        that this is a tape.

They lean forward into the sickly
warm wet wind of summer, pushing
the buggy full of child, she
spilling out of folds of cotton,
he bulging in his stripes, a home-made
crooked fag stuck in his mouth.

THERE WAS A DARKNESS IN THE AIR

There was a darkness in the air,
I looked and saw it speak,
felt it waiting by my back,
not savagery .... but near.

It was like an autumn slack
sharpening the air.
Its shadow shone beneath the black
as if the sun were there.

It muscled in, as meek
a line, as black and sleek
as lack of light, a smothered laugh,
a sudden lifted care.

It was ramrod straight
from standing still in fear.
The pain that chilled the hallway
had suffocated dare.

It was the father who was gone,
the wife who went before,
the brother who is never seen,
the sister at the door.

NOVEMBER

He trots in every morning
with the fluorescent mark
on his back. The first couple
of times, it was tentative,
after he'd fed with the ewes,
but now he appears by the
gate at the start of feeding
time. He gets plenty of maize
as well as black nuts, which
is what he likes. The hens go
bananas. There's always more
than enough both for him and
for them. He is so tiny
he doesn't look as if he'll
ever fatten up. He stands
apart always from the ewes,
even from his twin sister.
He cannot understand where
the three other wethers have
gone (they went to market in
Carlisle last week). He comes in
every morning full of hope
for his morning feed. One day
he will come in and be killed.
Will he know when that's to be?
Fool, you do not know when you
too will die, or even how.

TWO FEET IN A SACK

When you walk down the lane on a crisp winter's
morning following thick snow fall, hand in hand,
footprints behind, virgin snow around, and you
want to see your footprints and you look behind,
you have to stop, the footprints stop. What you find
is that you must twist around and your footprints
are smeared in the snow, lose the shape of your feet,
and you cannot move because your partner is
just standing there, is gazing at you fondly
wondering what you are doing, or, like you
is looking back. It's like two feet in a sack.
If one turns, the other can't stay back. We walked
down the lane holding hands. Our feet made prints in
the snow. I kept looking back, kept looking back.

DECEMBER (CHRISTMAS BOX)

We go feed the lambs. The wether
we were fattening for slaughter
is not there. I go look for him.
He lies apart. I stroke his head.
He stumbles to his feet. I drive
him to where the other lambs stand
and eat. He won't look at the food,
stood with his back to them. He has
a look of profound disgust in
his eyes. We bathe the ewe's feet. I
splash my eye. It stings. Snow swims in
shoals. We bury the lamb, go home.
We baptize him with a trickle
of water I coaxed from the stream
in a bucket. Stretched out and cold.
On the Horse Pasture, eyes open.
In the top far corner, on a
marshy piece of ground. Between the
stream and a marshy piece of ground.
With a crock of gold at each ear.
A rainbow hat to make a crock
of gold at each ear. A magic
dress for shepherding in the snow.
Gloves, striped green and blue. A velvet
and gold satin scarf. A magic
box of swords, a survival tool.
He lies apart. I stroke his head.

A NEW GROUND

We all went out on the field in the blustery wind,
Babs and Jakq and me and Cris and played
a game of dance (not fetch in case you thought –
no, this was something altogether other).
We joined our arms and sang and jumped.
And Babs was barking mad. And Jakq
raced after the ball, but let Babs have it,
the bully, but then Babs ran and rolled
and rubbed herself in shaggy clumps of grass
with ball in mouth till we were sure she must
have swallowed it. But up she sprang
and spat it at my feet. It bounced. We chased it
laughing, then the game began again.

JOSEPHINE DICKINSON, profoundly deaf from childhood, read classics at Oxford and then taught music for many years. She has had compositions performed in London, Devon and Orkney; and poems published in magazines. She lives with her husband in Cumbria, high in the Pennines, 'penning a few sheep in a gap of cloud'.

'As I write (March 27 2001), vets are investigating a farm in Alston for foot and mouth. I think everyone here accepts now that it is more or less inevitable we will all get it. But I have not given up hope. Alston Moor, with its rolling hills and fells, is not as famous as the Lakes but the effects on it should our animals succumb would be just as devastating. R S Thomas has a great poem, 'Reservoirs', in his 1968 collection. It is a lament for the Welsh language, but what is language but a code for everything that matters?'